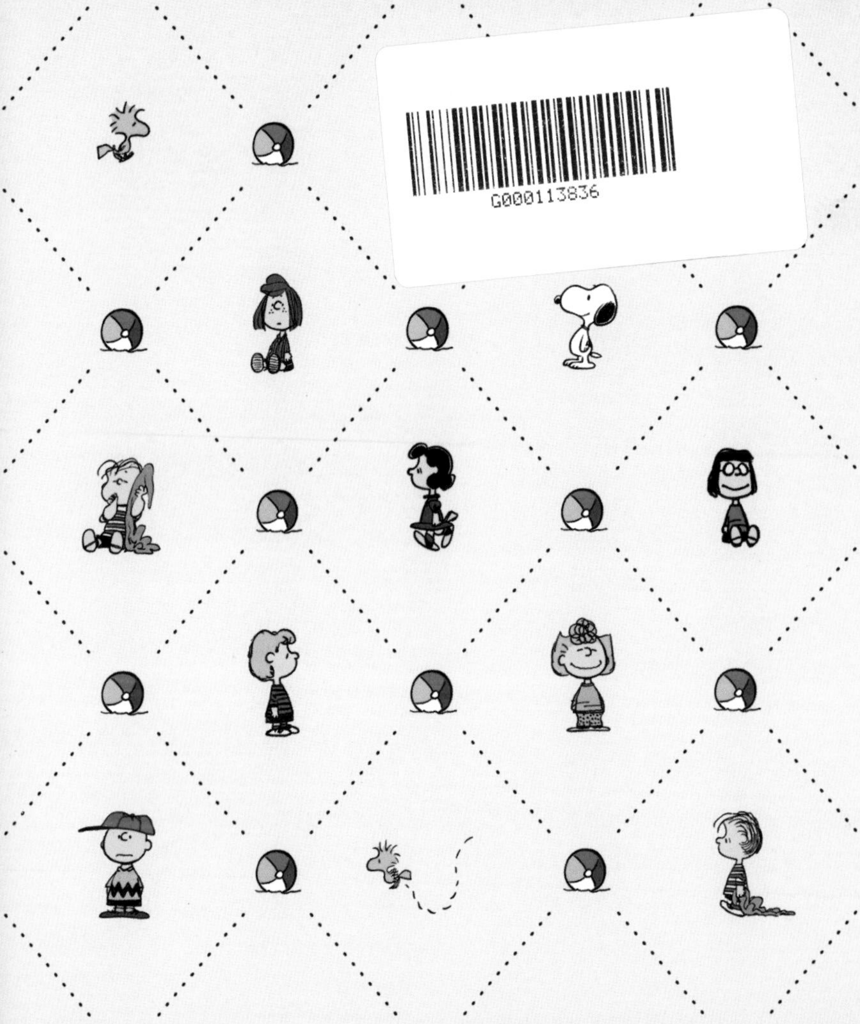

Published in Great Britain in 2016 by Canongate Books Ltd,
14 High Street, Edinburgh EH1 1TE

www.canongate.tv

1

British Library Cataloguing-in-Publication Data
A catalogue record for this book is available on
request from the British Library

ISBN 978 1 782 11369 0

PEANUTS written and drawn by Charles M. Schulz
Edited by Jenny Lord and Andy Miller
Design: Rafaela Romaya
Layout: Stuart Polson

Printed in China by C&C Offset Printing Co, Ltd

CHARLES M. SCHULZ

THE PEANUTS GUIDE TO
BROTHERS
AND SISTERS

CANONGATE

Edinburgh · London

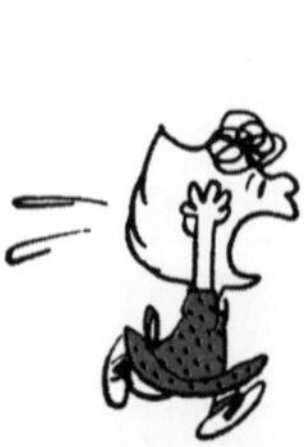

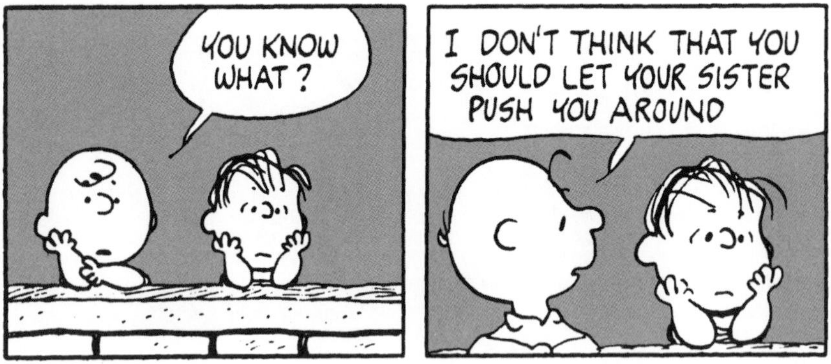
YOU KNOW WHAT?
I DON'T THINK THAT YOU SHOULD LET YOUR SISTER PUSH YOU AROUND

WHO CARES ABOUT PUSHING?
IT'S ALL THAT HITTING THAT GETS ME!

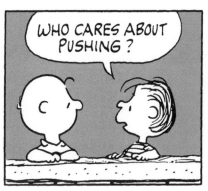

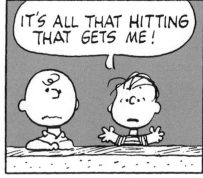

WHY ARE YOU SO CRABBY ALL THE TIME?
I SUPPOSE YOU'D RATHER HAVE A SISTER WHO IS SICKENINGLY SWEET AND ALL NICEY-NICEY...

POW!
I COULD STAND IT

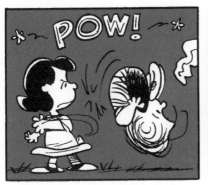

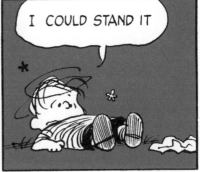

LITTLE BROTHERS
ARE BORN WITH
A SARCASM
THAT IS HANDED
DOWN FROM
GENERATION TO
GENERATION

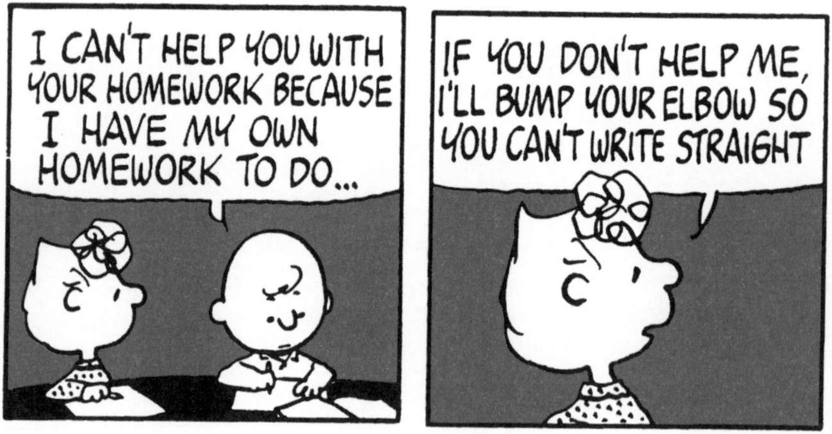
I CAN'T HELP YOU WITH YOUR HOMEWORK BECAUSE I HAVE MY OWN HOMEWORK TO DO...
IF YOU DON'T HELP ME, I'LL BUMP YOUR ELBOW SO YOU CAN'T WRITE STRAIGHT

I'LL BUMP YOUR NOSE!
THESE ARE EASY PROBLEMS

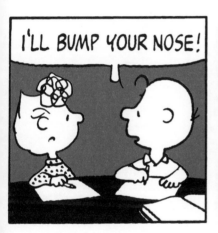

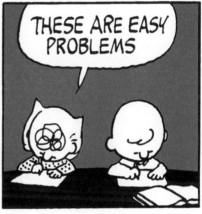

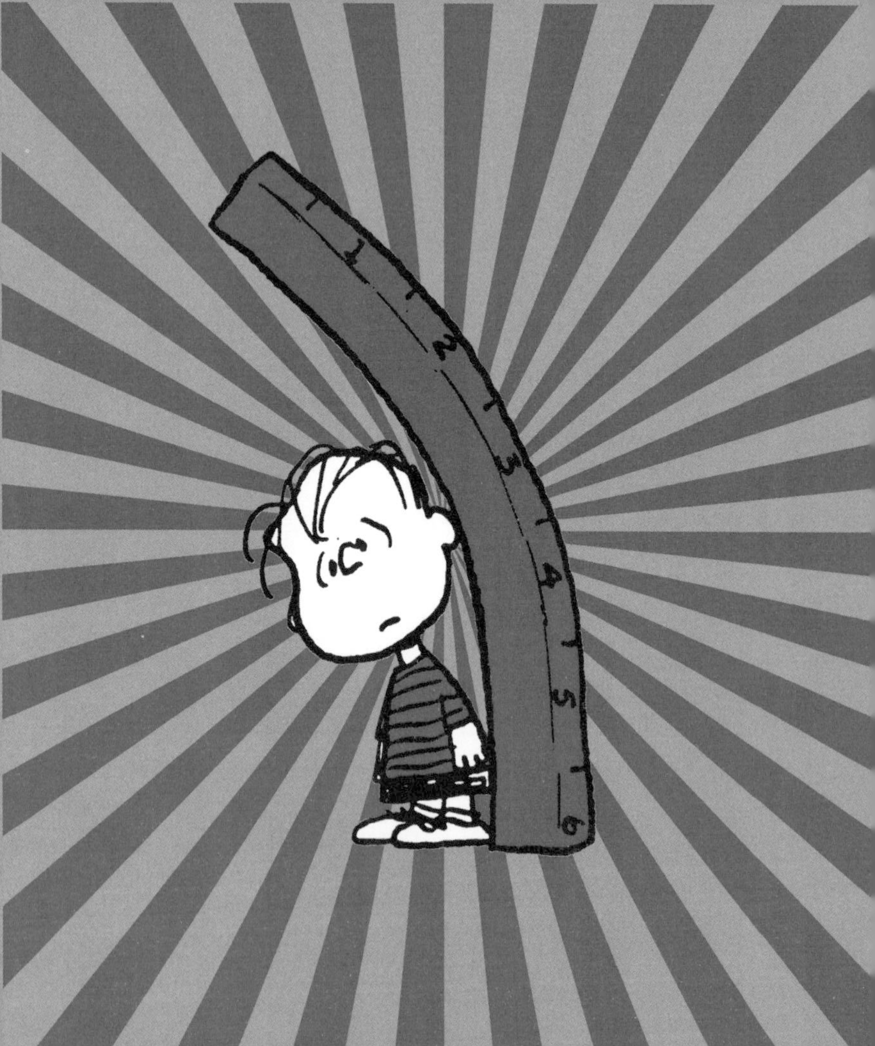
1
2
3
4
5
6

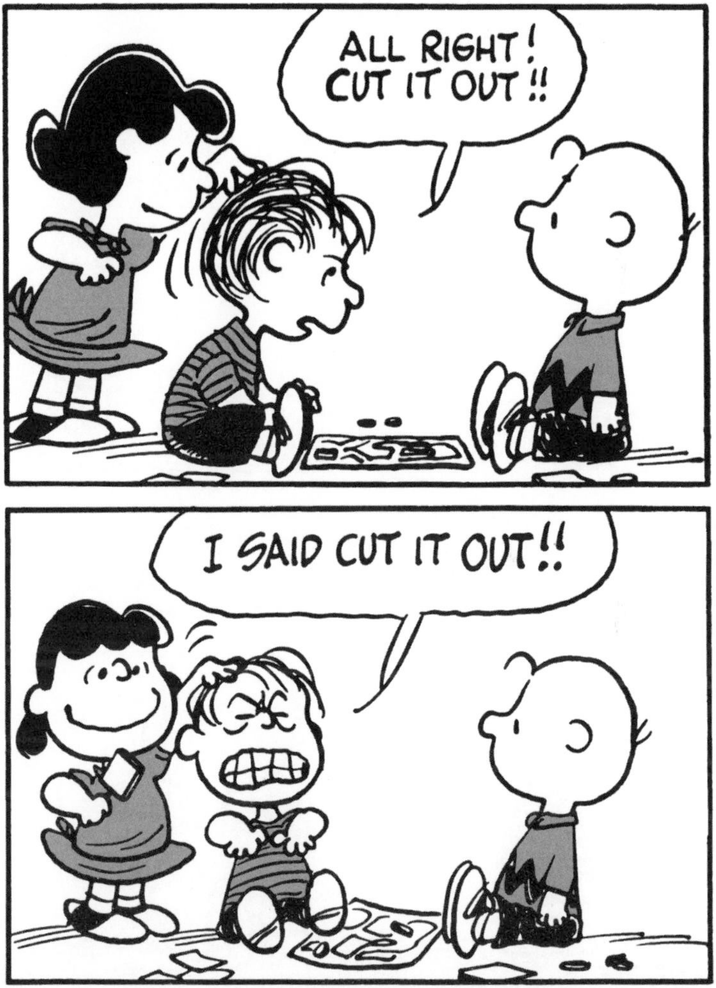
ALL RIGHT! CUT IT OUT!!
I SAID CUT IT OUT!!

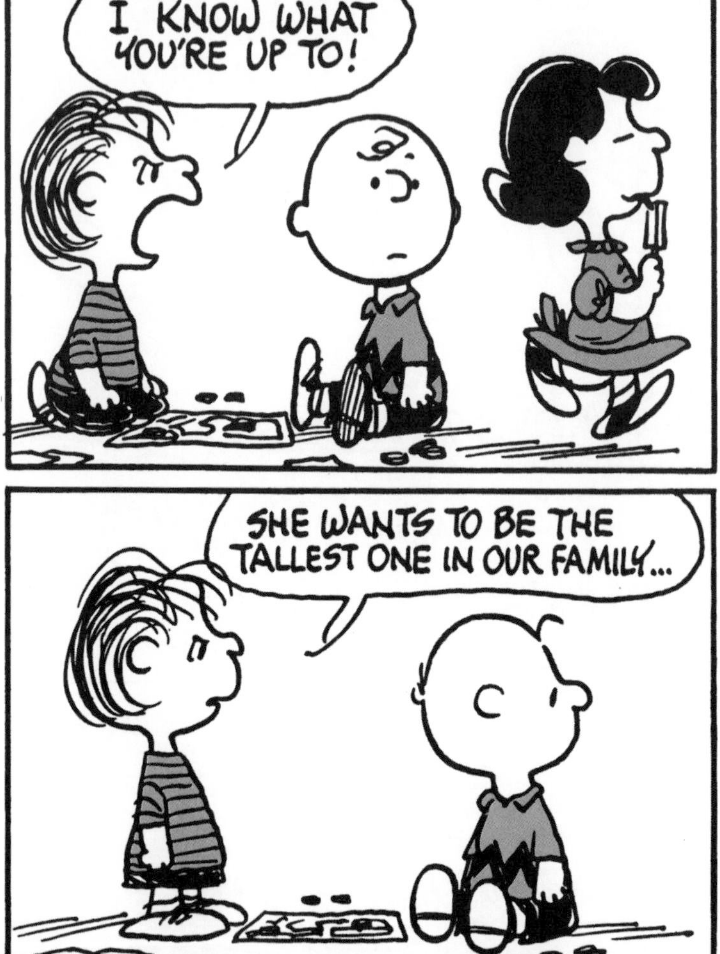
I KNOW WHAT YOU'RE UP TO!
SHE WANTS TO BE THE TALLEST ONE IN OUR FAMILY...

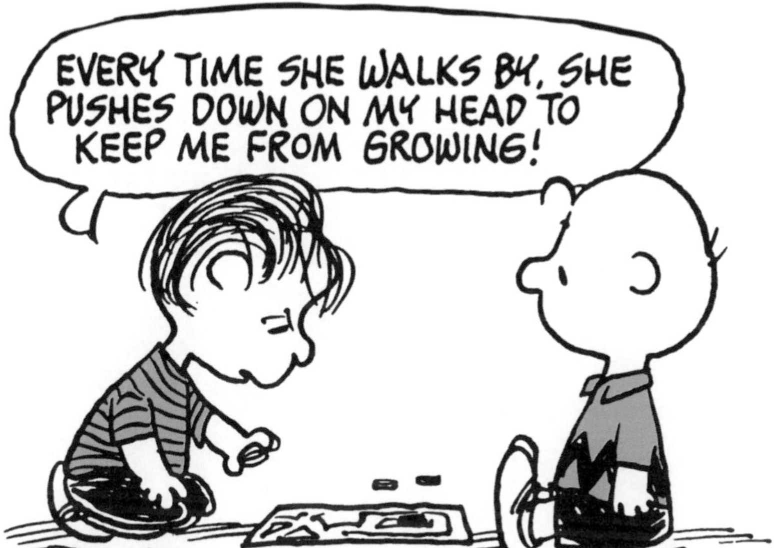
EVERY TIME SHE WALKS BY, SHE PUSHES DOWN ON MY HEAD TO KEEP ME FROM GROWING!

?
HEY! THIS DOG LOOKS LIKE BELLE!
BELLE? YOU KNOW BELLE?
SEE? HE LOOKS JUST LIKE THAT BEAGLE IN THE NEXT BLOCK...

BEAGLE?
BELLE!!!

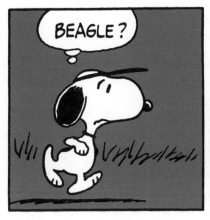

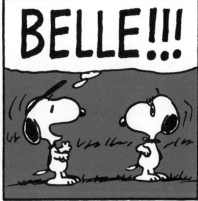

BROTHERS AND SISTERS SHOULD LEARN TO GET ALONG

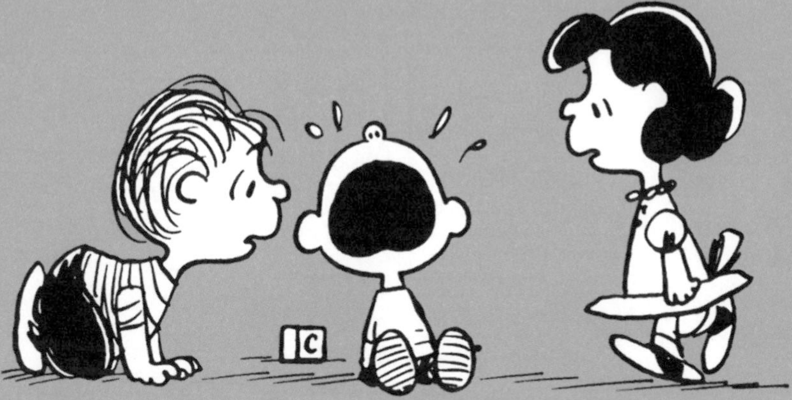
C

HI, IS CHUCK HOME?
WHO ARE YOU?
MY NAME IS MARCIE...I'M A FRIEND OF HIS FROM CAMP

MY BROTHER DOESN'T HAVE ANY FRIENDS
HOW CAN YOU SAY THAT? YOU DON'T EVEN KNOW ME..
NO, BUT I KNOW MY BROTHER!

THAT'S THE FUNNIEST THING I'VE EVER HEARD!
YOU THOUGHT YOU WERE RID OF **ME** AND NOW, INSTEAD OF HAVING **NO** BROTHERS, YOU HAVE **TWO** BROTHERS!! WHAT IRONY! WHAT SWIFT RETRIBUTION!

HA HA HA HA HA HA!
MY BLANKET AND I ARE LAUGHING OURSELVES SICK! WHAT IRONY!
HO HO HO HO HO HO!!

A FINE BROTHER YOU ARE!
JUST BECAUSE YOU WON'T HELP ME WITH MY HOMEWORK, I'M GOING TO FAIL!

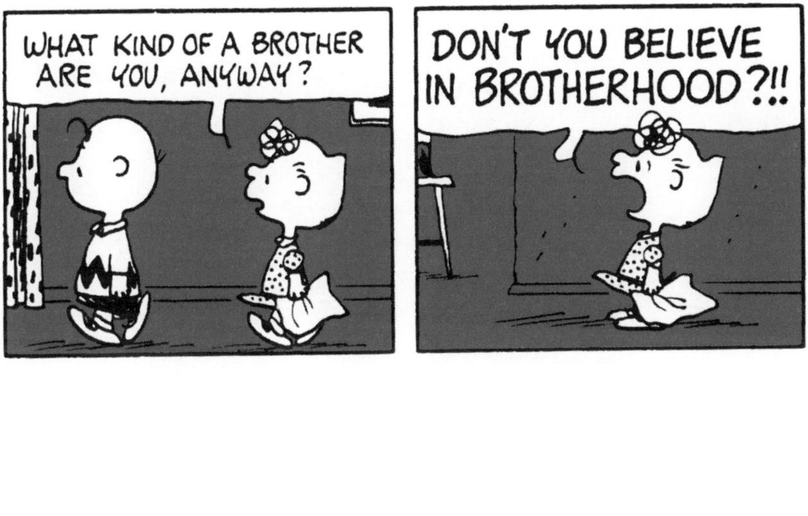
WHAT KIND OF A BROTHER ARE YOU, ANYWAY?
DON'T YOU BELIEVE IN BROTHERHOOD?!!

DID YOU HEAR ABOUT THE ORGANIZATION I'M FORMING?
IT'S GOING TO BE A CLUB FOR LITTLE BROTHERS LIKE MYSELF WHO ARE PERSECUTED BY DOMINEERING OLDER SISTERS, AND..

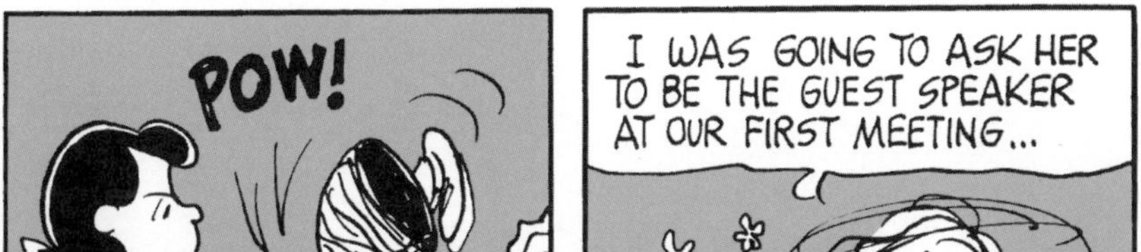
POW!
I WAS GOING TO ASK HER TO BE THE GUEST SPEAKER AT OUR FIRST MEETING...

LITTLE GIRLS
NEED
BIG BROTHERS

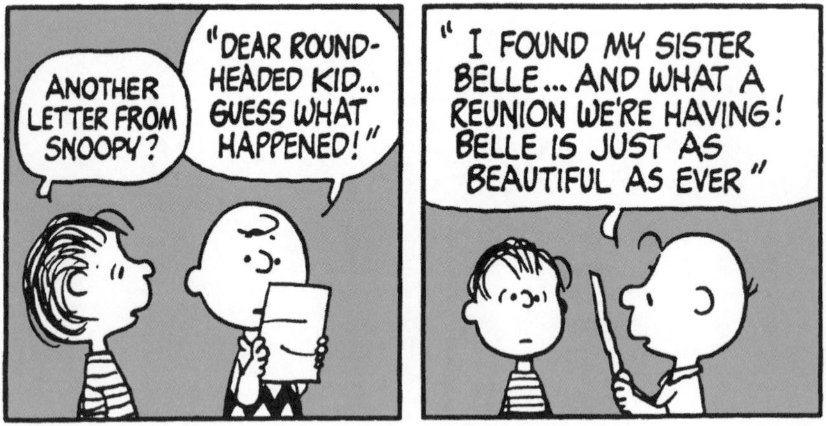
ANOTHER LETTER FROM SNOOPY?
"DEAR ROUND-HEADED KID... GUESS WHAT HAPPENED!"
" I FOUND MY SISTER BELLE... AND WHAT A REUNION WE'RE HAVING! BELLE IS JUST AS BEAUTIFUL AS EVER"

"UNFORTUNATELY, I CAN'T SAY MUCH FOR HER TEEN-AGE SON"

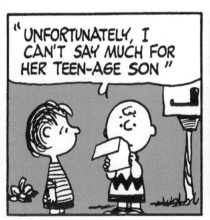

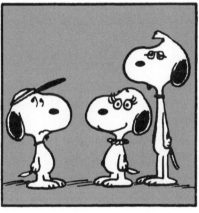

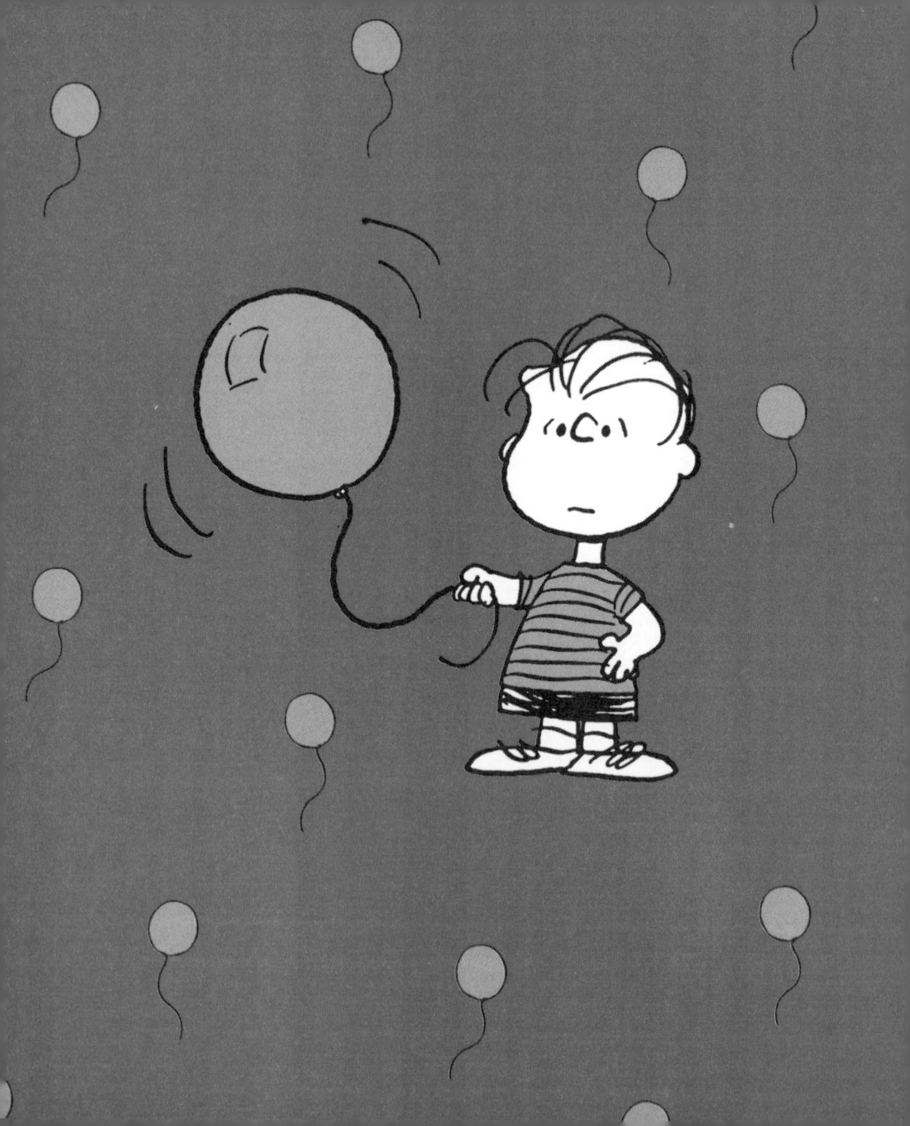

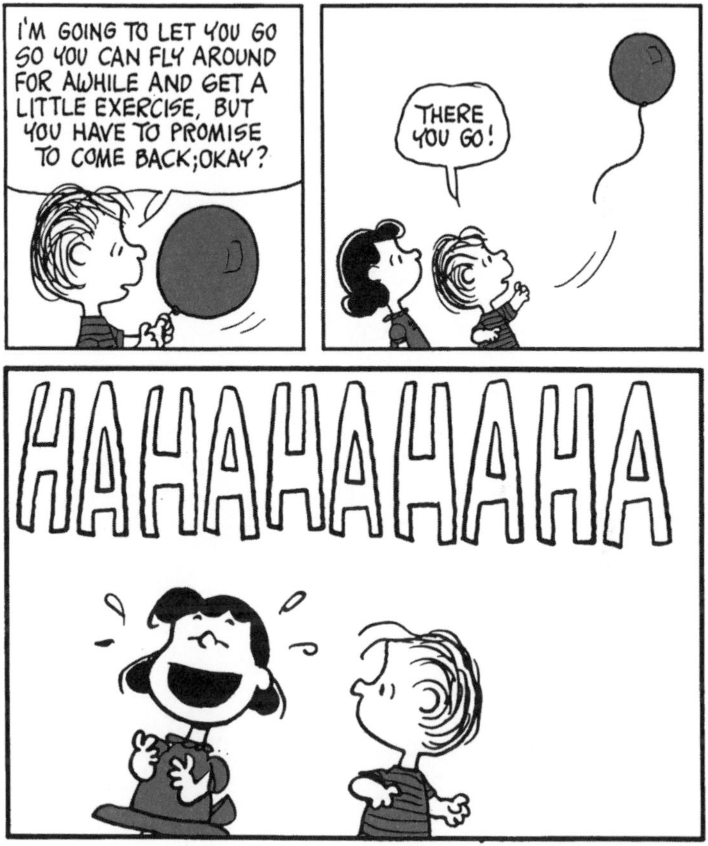
I'M GOING TO LET YOU GO SO YOU CAN FLY AROUND FOR AWHILE AND GET A LITTLE EXERCISE, BUT YOU HAVE TO PROMISE TO COME BACK; OKAY?
THERE YOU GO!
HAHAHAHAHAHA

BOY, IF YOU'RE NOT THE STUPIDEST PERSON ALIVE, I DON'T KNOW WHO IS! "FLY AROUND FOR AWHILE AND GET A LITTLE EXERCISE, AND THEN COME BACK!" A BALLOON? WOW!

BALLOONS AND LITTLE BROTHERS DRIVE ME CRAZY!

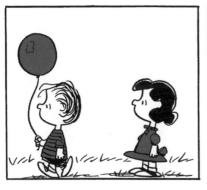

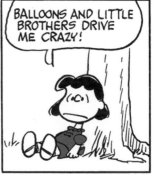

MY BEACH BALL! IT'S COMING BACK!
THAT KID ON THE OTHER SIDE OF THE WORLD SENT IT BACK! OUR NATIONS ARE IN HARMONY!
THE WIND CHANGED

TWO NATIONS, USING TWO INNOCENT CHILDREN AND A BEACH BALL, HAVE DEMONSTRATED TO THE WORLD THAT THEY CAN LIVE IN TOTAL HARMONY!
THE WIND CHANGED

YOUNGER
BROTHERS
LEARN TO
THINK FAST

HOW WOULD YOU LIKE TO SEE A LIST OF THINGS I WANT FOR CHRISTMAS?
ABSOLUTELY NOT! I WANT MY GIFT TO YOU THIS YEAR TO BE A COMPLETE AND DELIGHTFUL SURPRISE

WHAT A LOVELY GENEROUS THOUGHT...
SNIF
OFF THE OL' HOOKEROO!

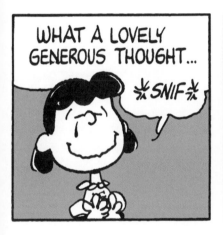

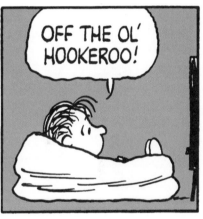

MY BROTHER HAS ARISEN!
EGGS BENEDICT FOR MY BROTHER, SPIKE!

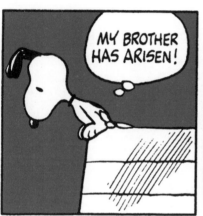

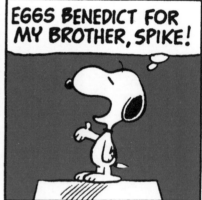

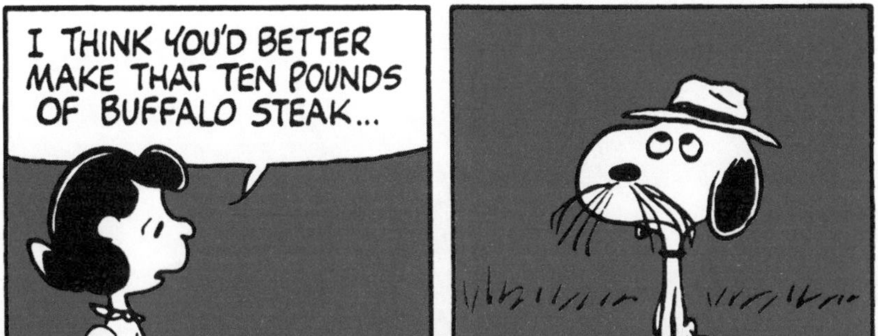
I THINK YOU'D BETTER MAKE THAT TEN POUNDS OF BUFFALO STEAK...

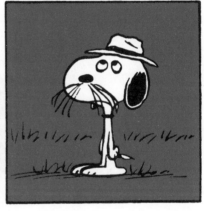

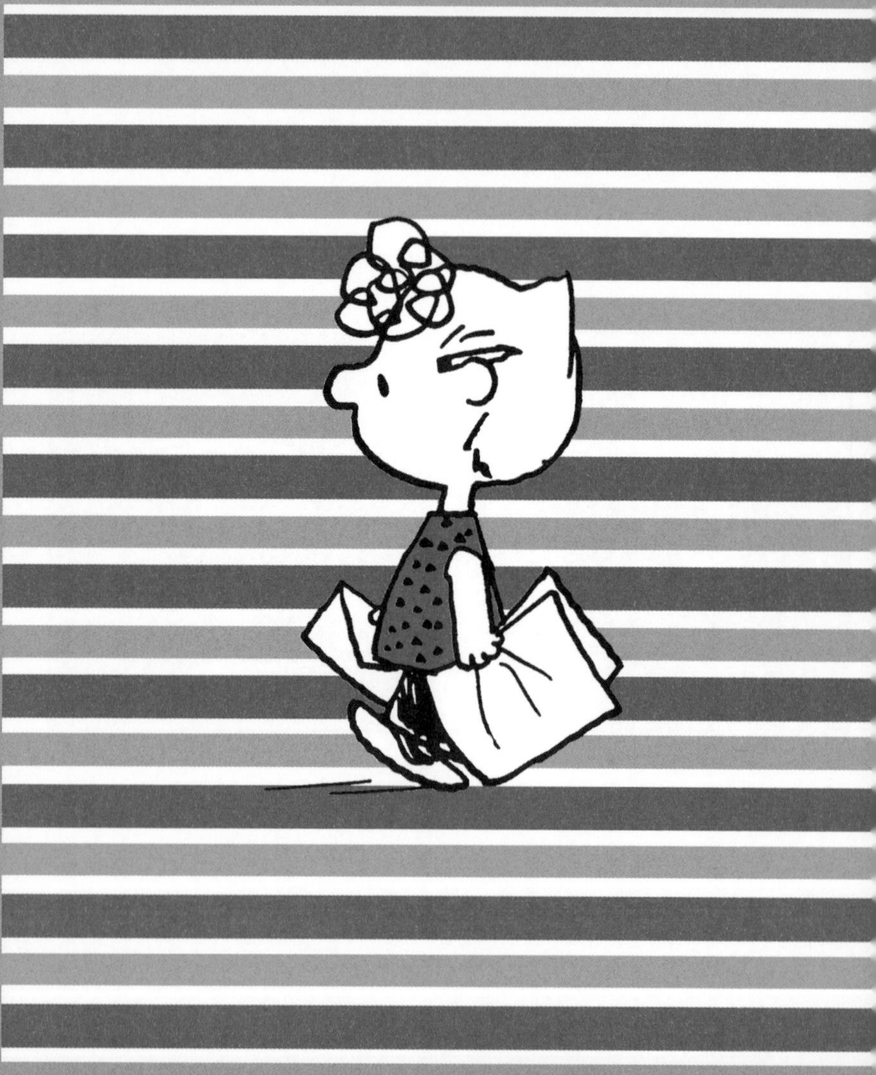

Dear Movie Critic,
How come you never like the same movies that I like?
You're weird! love, Sally Brown

Dear Book Critic,
What's the matter, can't you read? love, Sally Brown

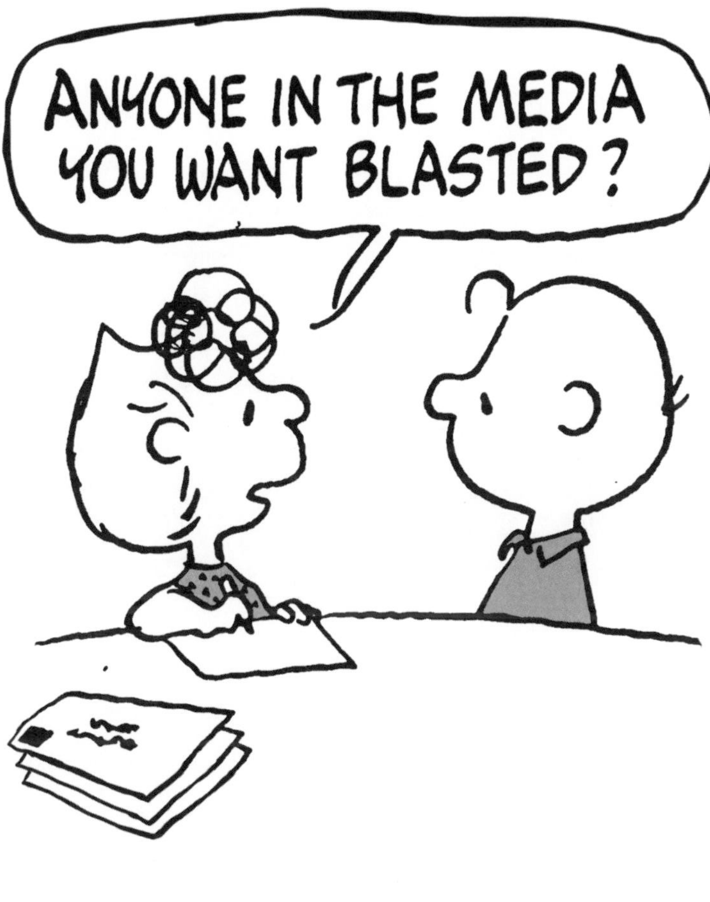
ANYONE IN THE MEDIA YOU WANT BLASTED?

SIGH
WHAT DID YOU SAY?
NOTHING, I JUST SIGHED
WELL, CUT IT OUT! IT BUGS ME!!

SIGH!

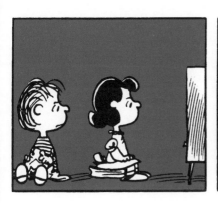

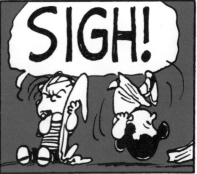

BIG SISTERS ARE THE CRAB GRASS IN THE LAWN OF LIFE!

I'M WRITING A STORY ABOUT SOME CAVE MEN
THEY'RE SITTING AROUND A CAMP FIRE, SEE, WHEN ALL OF A SUDDEN THEY'RE ATTACKED BY A HUGE THESAURUS!

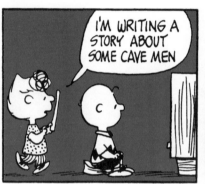

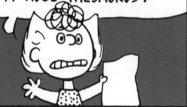

VOLUME ONE OR VOLUME TWO?
IT'S IMPOSSIBLE TO DISCUSS ANYTHING WITH A BIG BROTHER!

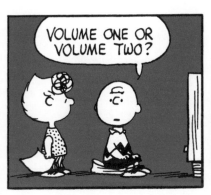

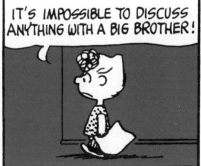

Z

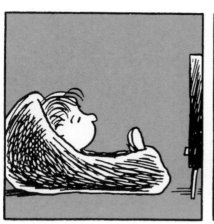

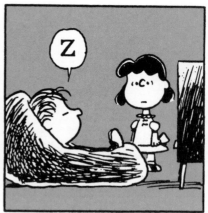

A FINE BROTHER YOU ARE! YOU LET ME MAKE A FOOL OUT OF MYSELF!!
?
IT ISN'T RAIN GEAR! IT'S REINDEER! WHY DIDN'T YOU TELL ME?!

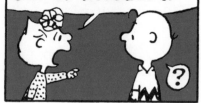

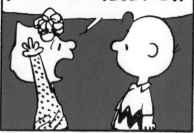

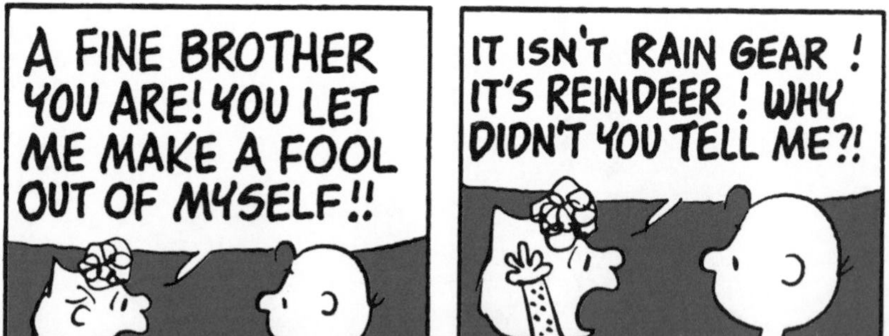

THEY ALL LAUGHED AT ME! EVEN THE TEACHER LAUGHED AT ME! I'LL NEVER BE ABLE TO GO TO THAT SCHOOL AGAIN!
POOR SWEET BABY...
SNIF!

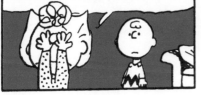

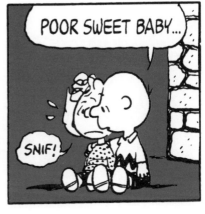

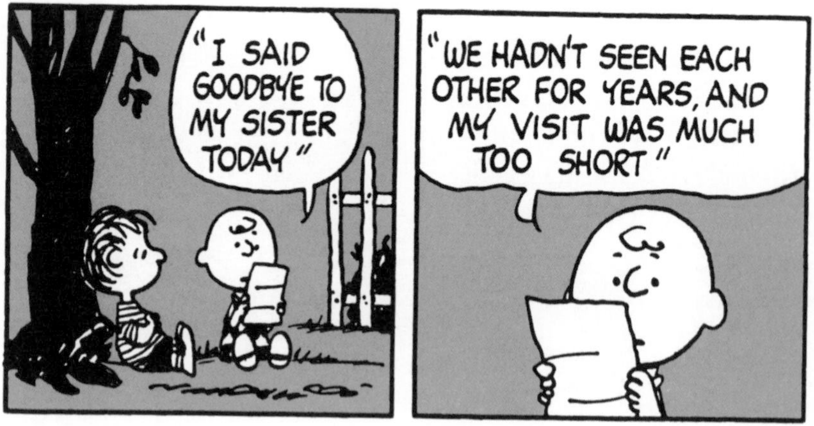
"I SAID GOODBYE TO MY SISTER TODAY"
"WE HADN'T SEEN EACH OTHER FOR YEARS, AND MY VISIT WAS MUCH TOO SHORT"

"NEEDLESS TO SAY, OUR FAREWELL WAS TEARFUL"
SNIF

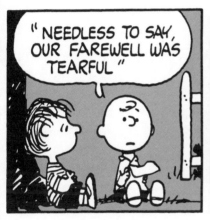

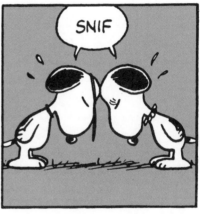

WHEN
BIG SISTERS
SPEAK LITTLE
BROTHERS
JUMP!

WHAT'S THIS I HEAR ABOUT YOU THROWING LINUS OUT OF THE HOUSE?
THAT'S NOT LEGAL, YOU KNOW.. HE'S PART OF YOUR FAMILY... LEGALLY, YOU CAN'T THROW HIM OUT..

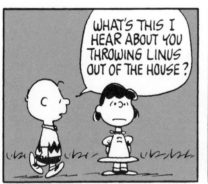

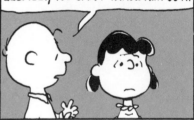

OH, YES, I CAN, AND I DID! LEGALLY, A BIG SISTER CAN THROW OUT A YOUNGER BROTHER BECAUSE SHE'S BIGGER THAN HE IS, AND HE BUGS HER ALL THE TIME, AND SHE CAN DO IT, AND I DID IT!!!
AND IF YOU'RE SMART, YOU WON'T GET INVOLVED!
I'M VERY SMART

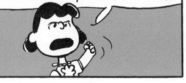

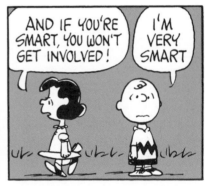

THIS IS A TREBLE CLEF
THIS IS AN AMPERSAND
&

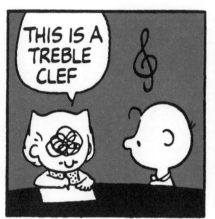

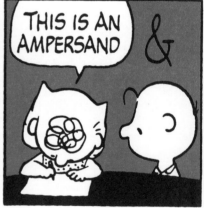

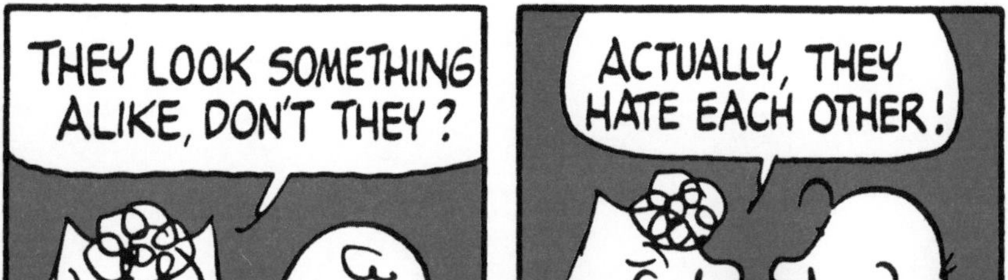
THEY LOOK SOMETHING ALIKE, DON'T THEY?
ACTUALLY, THEY HATE EACH OTHER!

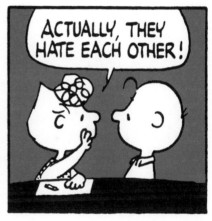

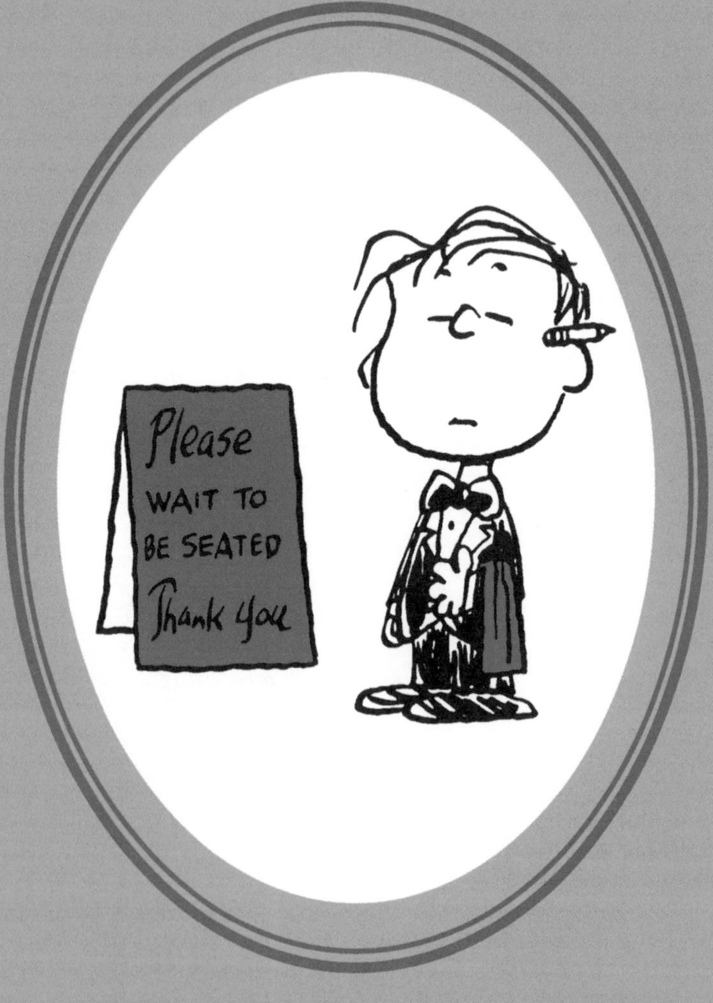
Please
WAIT TO
BE SEATED
Thank you

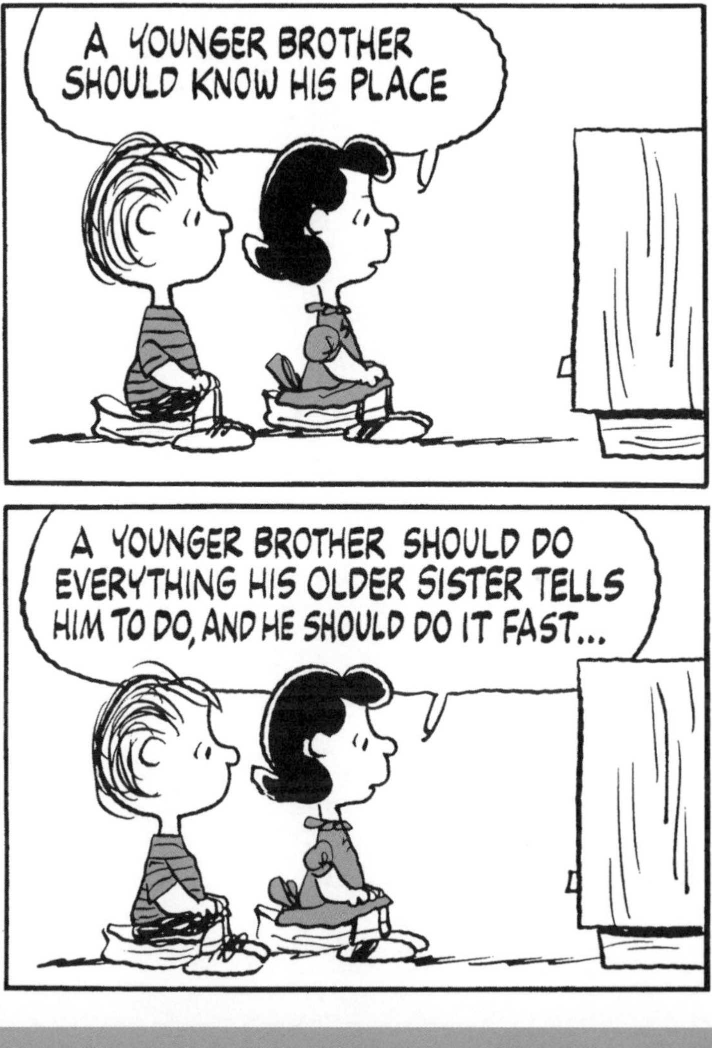
A YOUNGER BROTHER SHOULD KNOW HIS PLACE
A YOUNGER BROTHER SHOULD DO EVERYTHING HIS OLDER SISTER TELLS HIM TO DO, AND HE SHOULD DO IT FAST...

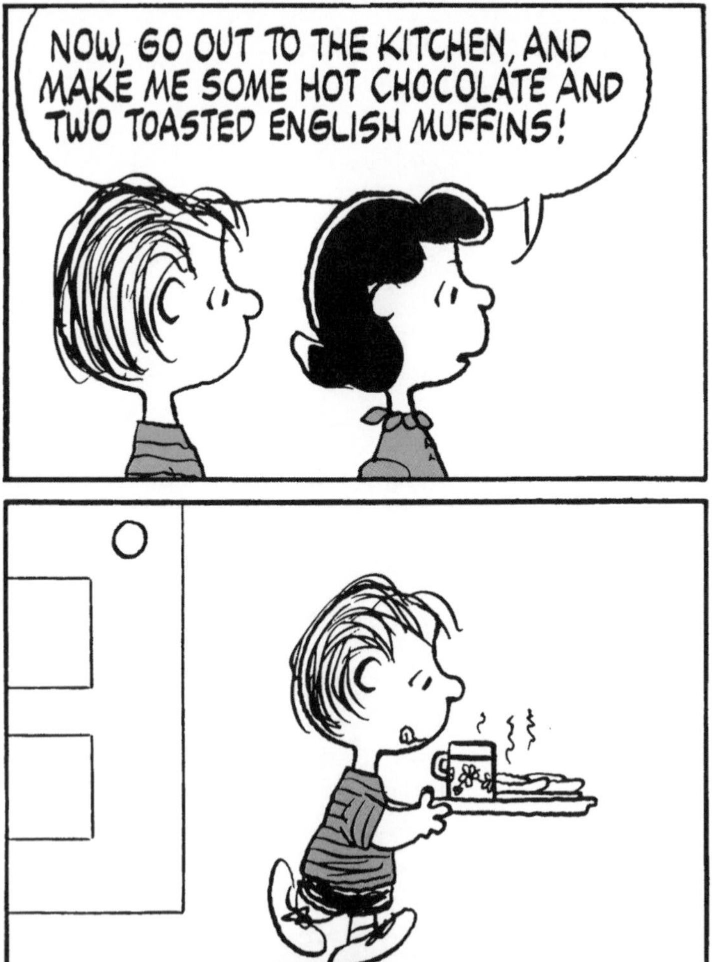
NOW, GO OUT TO THE KITCHEN, AND MAKE ME SOME HOT CHOCOLATE AND TWO TOASTED ENGLISH MUFFINS!

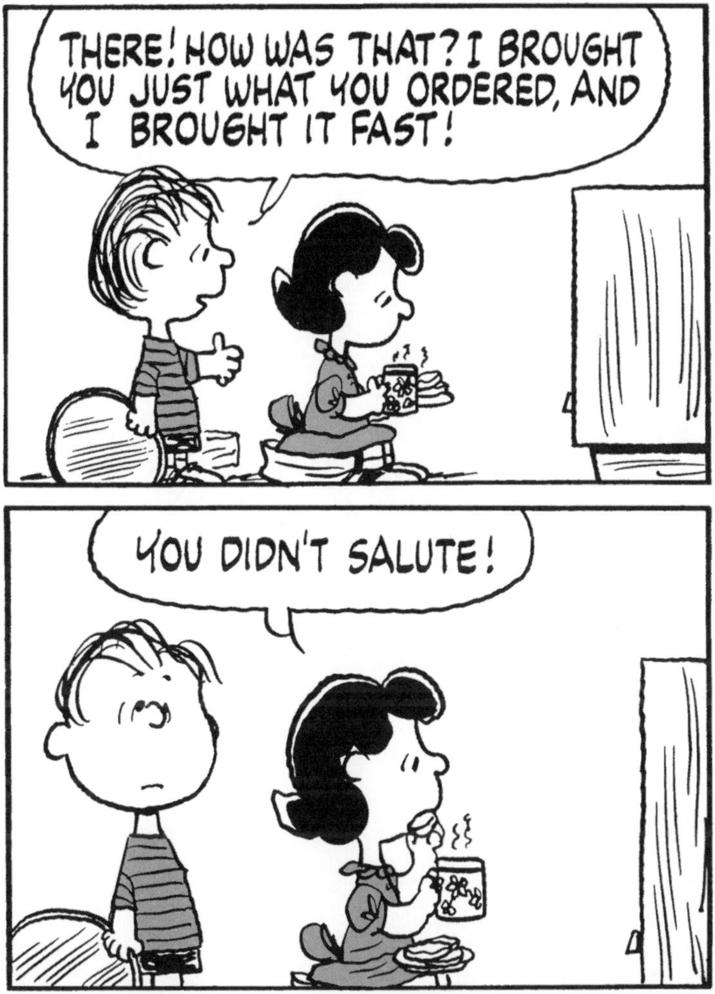
THERE! HOW WAS THAT? I BROUGHT YOU JUST WHAT YOU ORDERED, AND I BROUGHT IT FAST!
YOU DIDN'T SALUTE!

SCHOOL STARTS AGAIN NEXT WEEK...

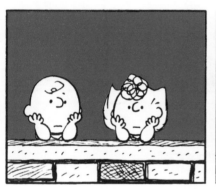

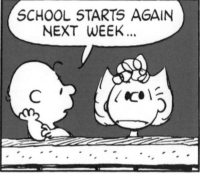

I THINK I'VE RUINED HER EYES FOR GOOD!

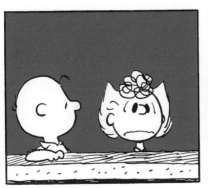

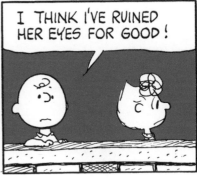

HERE'S A GENTLE REMINDER..

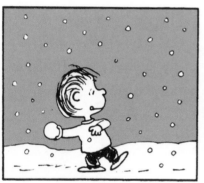

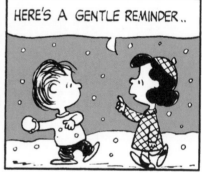

IF YOU THROW THAT SNOWBALL AT ME, I'LL BREAK EVERY BONE IN YOUR STUPID BODY!
SAVED BY A GENTLE REMINDER

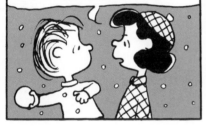

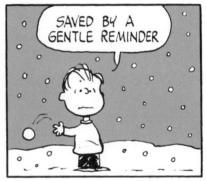

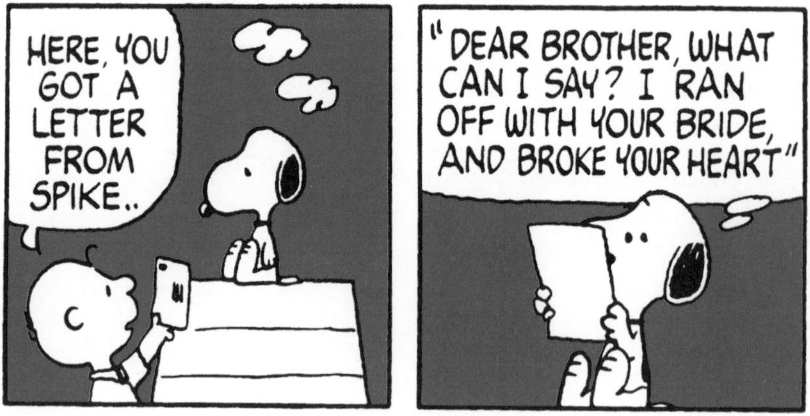
HERE, YOU GOT A LETTER FROM SPIKE..
"DEAR BROTHER, WHAT CAN I SAY? I RAN OFF WITH YOUR BRIDE, AND BROKE YOUR HEART"

"BUT YOU KNOW WHAT HAPPENED? THE DAY WE GOT HERE TO NEEDLES SHE LEFT ME, AND RAN OFF WITH A COYOTE!"
"HAVE YOU SEEN ANY GOOD MOVIES LATELY? YOUR BROTHER, SPIKE"

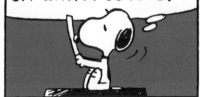

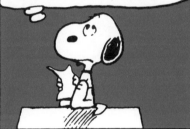

YOU HIT ME YESTERDAY, REMEMBER?
THEREFORE, I'VE DECIDED NOT TO GET YOU ANYTHING FOR CHRISTMAS THIS YEAR!

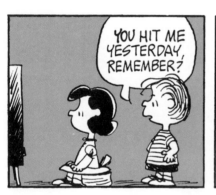

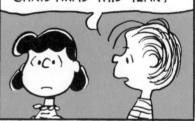

WHAT ARE YOU DOING??
TAKING BACK A HIT!

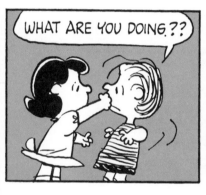

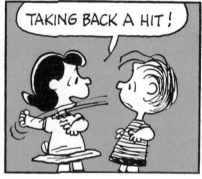

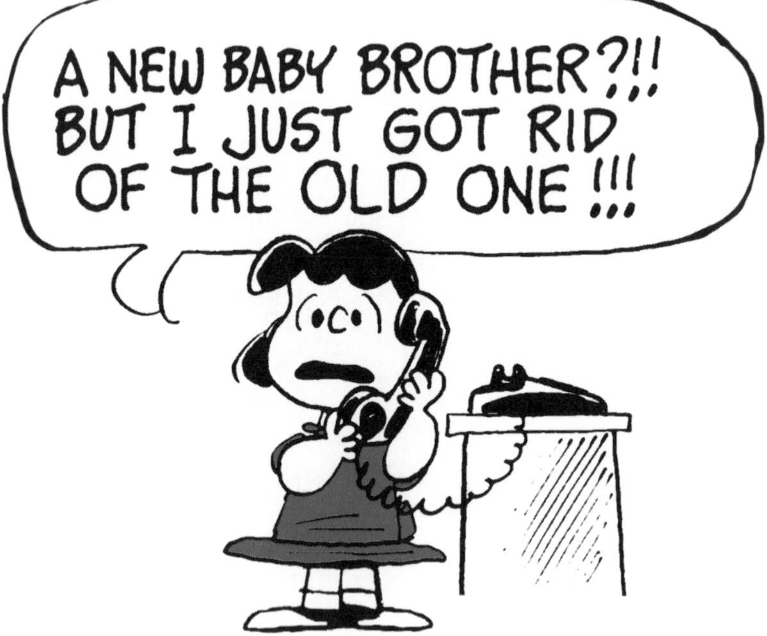
A NEW BABY BROTHER?!! BUT I JUST GOT RID OF THE OLD ONE!!!

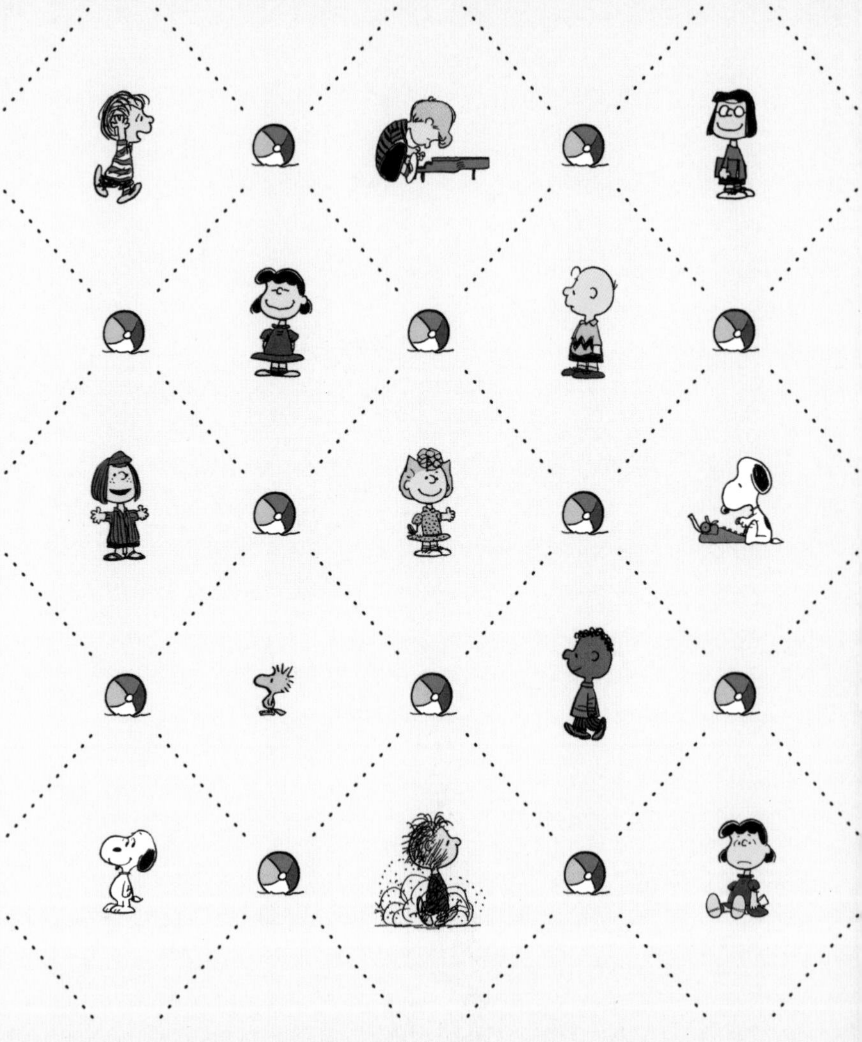